CLASSICAL SOLOS
FOR
ALTO SAXOPHONE

15 Easy Solos for Contest and Performance
Arranged by Philip Sparke

ONLINE MEDIA INCLUDED
Audio Recordings
Printable Piano Accompaniments

Speed • Pitch • Balance • Loop

To access recordings and PDF accompaniments visit:
www.halleonard.com/mylibrary

Enter Code
3141-1165-4958-8367

ISBN 978-1-70516-740-3

Visit Hal Leonard Online at
www.halleonard.com

World headquarters, contact:
Hal Leonard
7777 West Bluemound Road
Milwaukee, WI 53213
Email: info@halleonard.com

In Europe, contact:
Hal Leonard Europe Limited
1 Red Place
London, W1K 6PL
Email: info@halleonardeurope.com

In Australia, contact:
Hal Leonard Australia Pty. Ltd.
4 Lentara Court
Cheltenham, Victoria, 3192 Australia
Email: info@halleonard.com.au

WALTZ

Eb ALTO SAXOPHONE

MORITZ VOGEL
Arranged by PHILIP SPARKE

Allegro (♩ = 120)

rit.

00870093

CHORALE

Now praise, my soul, the Lord

E♭ ALTO SAXOPHONE

JOHANN SEBASTIAN BACH
Arranged by PHILIP SPARKE

3

00870093

HUMMING SONG

from *Album for the Young*

E♭ ALTO SAXOPHONE

ROBERT SCHUMANN
Arranged by PHILIP SPARKE

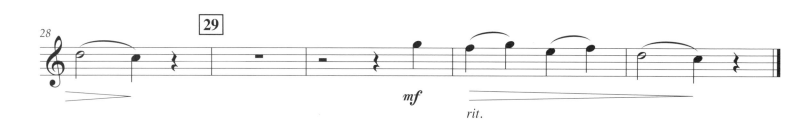

GYMNOPÉDIE NO. 1

ERIK SATIE
Arranged by PHILIP SPARKE

Eb ALTO SAXOPHONE

00870093

I'M CALLED LITTLE BUTTERCUP

from *HMS Pinafore*

E♭ ALTO SAXOPHONE

SIR ARTHUR SULLIVAN
Arranged by PHILIP SPARKE

STUDY
Op. 37, No. 3

HENRY LEMOINE
Arranged by PHILIP SPARKE

E♭ ALTO SAXOPHONE

00870093

MINUET
(Z. 649)

Eb ALTO SAXOPHONE

HENRY PURCELL
Arranged by PHILIP SPARKE

00870093

THEME AND VARIATION

from *Sonatina No. 3*

E♭ ALTO SAXOPHONE

THOMAS ATTWOOD
Arranged by PHILIP SPARKE

00870093

NORTHERN SONG

from *Album for the Young*

E♭ ALTO SAXOPHONE

ROBERT SCHUMANN
Arranged by PHILIP SPARKE

TWO GERMAN DANCES

from *Twelve German Dances, D. 420*

Eb ALTO SAXOPHONE

FRANZ SCHUBERT
Arranged by PHILIP SPARKE

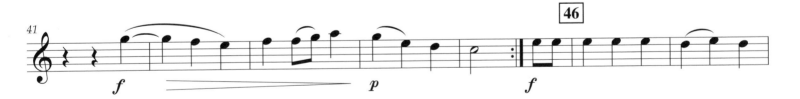

WATCHMAN'S SONG

from *Lyric Pieces, Op. 12*

Eb ALTO SAXOPHONE

EDVARD GRIEG
Arranged by PHILIP SPARKE

Moderato (♩ = 104)

GAVOTTE

Eb ALTO SAXOPHONE

JAN LADISLAV DUSSEK
Arranged by PHILIP SPARKE

Allegro (♩ = 120)

00870093

VIEN QUÀ, DORINA BELLA

E♭ ALTO SAXOPHONE

ANTONIO BIANCHI
Transcribed by **C. M. von WEBER**
Arranged by PHILIP SPARKE

MINUET

from *Notebook for Anna Magdalena Bach*

Eb ALTO SAXOPHONE

Attributed to **CHRISTIAN PETZOLD**
Arranged by PHILIP SPARKE

00870093

THE PRINCE OF DENMARK'S MARCH

from *Choice Lessons for the Harpsichord or Spinet*

E♭ ALTO SAXOPHONE

JEREMIAH CLARKE
Arranged by PHILIP SPARKE